D1355730

Books should be returned on or before the
last date stamped below

Golda MEIR

ANNA CLAYBOURNE

Heinemann
LIBRARY

www.heinemann.co.uk/library
Visit our website to find out more information about **Heinemann Library** books.

To order:
☎ Phone 44 (0) 1865 888066
▤ Send a fax to 44 (0) 1865 314091
▢ Visit the Heinemann Bookshop at www.heinemann.co.uk/library to browse our catalogue and order online.

First published in Great Britain by Heinemann Library, Halley Court, Jordan Hill, Oxford OX2 8EJ, part of Harcourt Education.

Heinemann is a registered trademark of Harcourt Education Ltd.

Produced for Heinemann by Discovery Books Ltd
Editorial: Patience Coster, Nicole Irving, Andrew Solway and Jennifer Tubbs
Design: Ian Winton
Illustrations: by Stefan Chabluk
Picture research: Rachel Tisdale
Production: Séverine Ribierre

Originated by Dot Gradations
Printed and bound in China by South China Printing Company

ISBN 0 431 13880 X
07 06 05 04 03
10 9 8 7 6 5 4 3 2 1

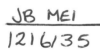

British Library Cataloguing in Publication Data
Claybourne, Annna
  Golda Meir. – (Leading Lives)
  956.9'4'053'092

A full catalogue record for this book is available from the British Library.

Acknowledgements
The publishers would like to thank the following for permission to reproduce photographs:
Anthony Potter Collection/Hulton Archive: p. **29**; Bettmann/Corbis: pp. **4, 36, 37**; Corbis: pp. **34, 54**; David Rubinger/Corbis: pp. **44, 48, 52**; Golda Meir Library: pp. **5, 7, 16, 17, 18**; Hulton Archive: pp. **23, 26, 33**; Hulton Deutsch Collection/Corbis: p. **31**; Hulton Getty: pp. **9, 43**; Milwaukee County Historical Society: p. **15**; Popperfoto: pp. **20, 39, 49, 51, 53**; Richard T. Nowitz/Corbis: p. **10**; Topham Picturepoint: pp. **6, 13, 40, 46**.

Cover photograph of Golda Meir reproduced with permission of Popperfoto.

Every effort has been made to contact copyright holders of any material reproduced in this book. Any omissions will be rectified in subsequent printings if notice is given to the publishers.

Disclaimer
All the Internet addresses (URLs) given in this book were valid at the time of going to press. However, due to the dynamic nature of the Internet, some addresses may have changed, or sites may have ceased to exist since publication. While the author and publishers regret any inconvenience this may cause readers, no responsibility for any such changes can be accepted by either the author or the publishers.

Contents

Any words appearing in the text in bold, **like this**, are explained in the Glossary.

1 Woman on a mission

The year was 1969, and the USA was preparing for a grand state visit. Banquet menus were planned, bands rehearsed, and the red carpet was rolled out at the White House. When the guest of honour arrived, a crowd of more than 30,000 people had gathered to greet her. Wherever she went, she was hailed as a hero. Her name was Golda Meir.

◀ *Golda Meir with President Nixon during her state visit to the USA in 1969. Although Nixon was later forced out of office amid a series of scandals, Golda always supported him in return for his help when she became Israel's prime minister.*

In her youth, Meir had lived in the USA in Milwaukee, Wisconsin. Now she was leader of the young state of Israel, in the Middle East. She had come back to the USA, which was a supporter of Israel, to ask for help. Her country was engaged in constant **skirmishes** with its neighbours, and needed money and arms to defend its borders.

Leading the way

Golda Meir was not everyone's idea of a world leader. A small lady of 70, she was already a grandmother when she took over the leadership of Israel in March 1969. At first she had taken the job temporarily, after the death of Prime Minister Levi Eshkol. She had planned to stand in until elections could

▶ *Students welcoming Prime Minister Meir to her old hometown of Milwaukee in 1969.*

be held later that year. Her colleagues persuaded her to stay on and she was to lead Israel for more than five years.

At the time, Meir was only the second woman in the world to be elected prime minister in any country (after Sirimavo Bandaranaike, who became Sri Lanka's leader in 1960). Not only did she lead Israel – she was also one of the people who had helped to found the new country just twenty years earlier.

Strong beliefs

All her life, Golda Meir wanted one thing more than any other – to create a peaceful **homeland** for her people, the Jews. She struggled endlessly to make that dream a reality. She was driven by her heartfelt belief in the rights of the Jewish people, and helped by her incredible energy. Her stubborn devotion to her task made her many enemies. Yet her iron will and powerful **charisma** made her one of the most effective natural leaders in history.

Woman at the top

Golda Meir never felt that being a woman should stop her from succeeding. During her political career, interviewers often asked her how it felt to be a woman minister. She would reply innocently: 'I don't know – I've never been a man minister.'

Golda Meir spent the first eight years of her life in Russia. She was born Golda Mabovitch on 3 May 1898 in Kiev (now part of Ukraine). When she was three, her family moved to Pinsk (now in Belarus).

Golda's father, Moshe Mabovitch, was a carpenter and her mother Blume was employed to look after other people's children, as well as looking after her own. But they were still very poor. Later in life, Meir remembered that during her childhood 'there was never enough of anything…. I was always a little too cold outside and a little too empty inside.' She hated having to share her food with her baby sister, Zipke. Their big sister, Shenya, often fainted from hunger. The family lived in a single room. These terrible living conditions meant that five of the Mabovitches' children – four boys and a girl – died before they reached their first birthdays. Only Shenya, Golda and Zipke survived.

◀ This picture taken in Putilov, Russia, shows the dirty and cramped conditions in which many poorer members of society lived at the end of the 19th century.

Discrimination

One reason life was so hard was that Golda and her family were Jewish. Jews were an **ethnic minority** in Russia, with their own religion and traditions; because they were different, many people hated and feared them. Jews were forced to live in their own areas, away from other Russians, who were mainly Christians. Although he was a good carpenter, it was hard for Golda's father to find work because people did not want to employ Jews and **discriminated** against them.

The pogroms

Worst of all, large numbers of Jewish people were massacred in violent attacks called **pogroms**. Gangs of rioters would charge through Jewish areas, attacking, wounding and even killing Jewish people and destroying their homes. The **Tsar** (the Russian ruler) turned a blind eye to the pogroms, and his **cossacks** (soldiers) sometimes even joined in.

Golda was terrified by the pogroms, but also deeply puzzled. Why would anyone want to hurt her just because of her religion and culture? When she saw her father boarding up their front door because of the pogroms, she was angry. It was no good simply to hide away. Even as a small child, Golda believed there had to be a better way for Jewish people to save themselves from this nightmare.

▲ *Golda Mabovitch as a child in 1904, aged six.*

A cossack attack

When Golda was five and living in Pinsk, she went to play with friends near a swamp called the *blotte*. A band of cossacks came galloping towards them on their horses. Instead of stopping, they rode straight over the crouching children, not caring if they trampled them to death. Golda survived, but she never went near the *blotte* again.

The horror of a pogrom

'It is impossible to account the amounts of goods destroyed in a few hours. The hurrahs of the rioting. The pitiful cries of the victims filled the air. Wherever a Jew was met he was savagely beaten into insensibility. One Jew was dragged from a streetcar and beaten until the mob thought he was dead. The air was filled with feathers and torn bedding. Every Jewish household was broken into and the unfortunate Jews in their terror endeavored to hide in cellars and under roofs.'
(An eyewitness account of a pogrom in Kishinev, Russia in April 1903, printed in the *New York Times*.)

An American dream

In 1903, disheartened with his failure to make a good living in Russia, Moshe Mabovitch decided to go to the USA. He was sure it would be easier to find work there, and he could save money and send it home to his family. Meanwhile, Blume and the three girls were to stay with Blume's parents in Pinsk.

At that time, people from all over the world, including more than one million Jews, were going to America to make their fortunes. They believed they could find better lives for themselves and for their families. Although many people did build better lives, it wasn't always as easy as they expected. Golda's father struggled for three years before finding a good enough job to support his family. Left behind in Pinsk, they only survived with help from Golda's grandfather. They moved in above a bakery, and Golda's mother got a job there. Life was still hard.

Shenya's secrets

As she grew older, Golda realized that Shenya was keeping secrets from the rest of her family. Shenya was nine years older than Golda, and already a teenager. She would disappear to mysterious meetings and come home late. She had huge arguments with her mother, who seemed terrified for her safety.

Hiding on top of the stove, or pretending to be asleep, Golda would eavesdrop when her sister's friends came to the house, in an effort to find out what they were talking about. She discovered that Shenya was a member of a political movement that wanted to make things better for the Jews. Sometimes they talked about overthrowing the Tsar, but mostly they dreamed of starting a new, independent state for Jews to live in. This idea was growing among Jewish people around the world, and it was called **Zionism** after Zion, an old Hebrew word for the Jewish people and their **homeland**.

In Russia, it was against the law to be a member of a Zionist group. If Shenya had been caught, she would have been arrested and punished by the police. Blume Mabovitch was very afraid for her daughter, but she couldn't persuade her to give up her political activities. So, in 1905, she wrote to her husband saying that they had to leave Russia. They were going to join him in America.

◀ *Immigrants awaiting medical examination on arrival at Ellis Island, New York, 1904. Most people who moved to the USA from Europe had to be processed here before being allowed to enter the country.*

From an early age, Golda Meir realized that she was in a minority. Although her family was not especially religious, Jewish culture and traditions played a big part in their lives. Instead of the Christian festivals most Russians and Europeans celebrated, they celebrated Jewish holidays, such as Passover, Hanukah and Yom Kippur. Golda's family also spoke in a traditional Jewish language called **Yiddish**, and ate only kosher food. According to the religious laws of keeping kosher, some foods, such as shellfish and pork, are forbidden.

◀ In 1993, a Jewish family in the Negev region of Israel celebrate Passover with a special meal called the Passover Seder. Passover is one of the most important Jewish festivals.

In Russia, Jewish people were only allowed to live in a certain area of the country (known as the Pale of Settlement). They also lived in specific Jewish areas within each town, called **ghettos**. The ghettos were crowded and had poor housing, but they gave Jewish people a strong sense of belonging to their own, unique community. Their traditional recipes, folk music and religious rituals had been handed down over hundreds of years. Jewish people only socialized among their own kind, and only married other Jews. It was in this kind of close-knit atmosphere that Golda Meir grew up.

'Next year in Jerusalem'

Every year, in common with most Jews, Golda and her family celebrated the Jewish festival of Passover, which remembers the **exodus** of Jews from Egypt where they were slaves. The story of the Jews' desire for freedom is read during Passover and the words 'L'shanah ha-baah bi Yerushalayim' – 'Next year in Jerusalem' – are chanted. This is because, more than 2000 years ago, the Jewish people had

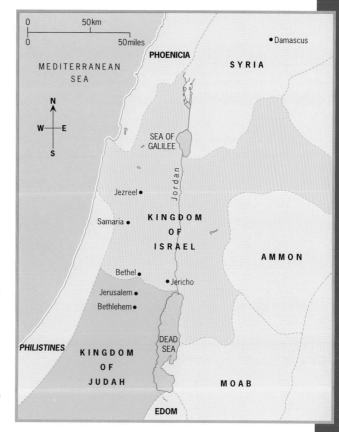

▲ This map shows the original Jewish homeland in around 800 BCE. It was split into two areas, one called Israel and the other called Judah.

their own kingdom centred on the holy city of Jerusalem. According to the Bible, God promised this land to the Jews, or **Hebrews** as they were known, as their own.

However, because of various wars and conquests, most Jews were eventually forced to leave the area. Golda's ancestors ended up in Russia, but Jews settled in many countries, especially in Eastern Europe. This scattering of Jewish people around the world is called the Jewish **diaspora**. Although they made new lives elsewhere, most Jews preserved their traditional culture and beliefs, and continued to view Jerusalem as their spiritual home – a home to which, one day, they would return.

Time to go home?

Golda Meir was born at the end of the 19th century. In earlier centuries, most Jews had held a traditional belief that their **Messiah**, or divine leader, would appear and lead them back to the **Promised Land**. But by Golda's time, ideas had begun to change. People started saying that, instead of waiting for a Messiah, Jews should make the return to the Promised Land themselves. At that time, the old land of the Hebrews was called Palestine, and was part of the **Ottoman Empire**, which was controlled by Turkey. Perhaps it could be turned back into a **homeland** for the Jews?

FOR DETAILS ON KEY PEOPLE OF MEIR'S TIME, SEE PAGE 58.

A movement begins

Many people felt there was an urgent need for a Jewish homeland because anti-Semitism – hatred of Jews – was causing so much suffering. For centuries other groups, especially Christians, had disliked the Jews and accused them of being mean, dishonest and simply being 'different'. Now the prejudice and **persecution** seemed to be growing even worse. Around Europe, Jews like Golda's sister, Shenya, discussed what should be done, and the plan for a homeland began to take shape.

A Hungarian Jew named Theodor Herzl wrote a booklet called *The Jewish State*. In 1897, at a Jewish conference in Basle, Switzerland, he founded a society called the World **Zionist** Organization, which planned to find a Jewish homeland. By 1900, **Zionism** was a major force in Eastern Europe, and the first European Jews had already started moving to Palestine to settle there.

Theodor Herzl

Theodor Herzl was born in Hungary in 1860. He moved to Vienna, the capital of Austria. From there he worked as a newspaper correspondent in Paris, France. Herzl was outraged by the anti-Semitism he witnessed. He wrote books and organized conferences devoted to the creation of a Jewish state. He was a hero to young Zionists in the early 20th century, when Golda Meir and her sisters were growing up. After Herzl died in 1904, many Jews 'sat shiva' – a traditional period of mourning for seven days. Golda's sister, Shenya, wore black mourning clothes for two years.

▲ *Theodor Herzl (centre) and some of his followers on their way to Palestine in 1898.*

A new world

Golda would one day go to Palestine herself. Before that, however, there was another huge move to make. She and her family were preparing to leave their old life behind, and join Moshe in Milwaukee, USA.

Today, it is possible to fly from Europe to the USA in a few hours. But in 1906, for a poor family from Russia, the journey took weeks. First, Golda's mother had to bribe the police to let them leave Russia. When they reached Galicia (now part of Poland), they had to hide in a freezing cold shack for two days, waiting for a train to take them to the coast. After waiting another two days in Belgium, they finally boarded a ship for the fourteen-day journey across the Atlantic. They travelled in **steerage**, the lowest and cheapest class, with eight people crammed into each tiny cabin.

Culture shock

Throughout the journey, Golda wondered what Milwaukee would be like. But the reality was beyond anything she could have imagined. She was overwhelmed and amazed by the USA – the huge buildings, the amazing variety of shops to visit and things to buy, the bright colours of street advertisements and people's clothes. Golda had never seen so many vehicles on the streets – she had never even been in a car before. She loved it.

However, it was difficult for the family to live together again after so long. Moshe had changed. He had new American friends and clothes, and had learned English. He wanted his family to change too. Golda and Zipke were young enough to accept this, but Shenya hated it. She had been forced to leave her boyfriend, Shamai, behind in Pinsk, and she missed her home terribly.

Settling in

Although they were still poor, life was easier in the USA. Moshe had found work with a railway company, and Blume decided to set up her own general store. Golda started at school, which she loved, and made a new best friend called Regina Hamburger. There were lots of Jewish people in Milwaukee, and this friendly community embraced the Mabovitch family.

▲ *Milwaukee in the early 20th century. To eight-year-old Golda Mabovitch, who had spent her life in poverty and had never seen a tall building or ridden in a car, it seemed like a different universe.*

Memories of Milwaukee

In her autobiography, *My Life*, Golda Meir wrote about her amazement and excitement when she arrived in the USA. 'I was delighted by my pretty new clothes, by the soda pop and ice cream... ' she recalled. 'Everything looked so colourful and fresh, as though it had just been created.'

Politics and Palestine

By the early 1900s, many East European Jews, including those now in Milwaukee, were talking about **Zionism**. The Mabovitches' small apartment was always full of friends and neighbours, discussing and debating the Palestine issue over endless glasses of tea. Influenced by these discussions, Golda found herself thinking about Zionism more and more. She knew that increasing numbers of Jews were moving to Palestine to start a Jewish **homeland** there. And she knew that some day she would like to join them.

Running away

Shenya caught **tuberculosis** and was sent hundreds of kilometres away, to Denver, Colorado, to recover. She set up home there with Shamai, who had come to the USA to be with her. At home in Milwaukee, the teenage Golda became increasingly annoyed with her parents. They wanted her to work in their shop and marry a man who was twice her age. But Golda wanted to stay at school. How could she help to build a Jewish state if she didn't have a good education?

▼ *Golda Mabovitch at school in 1912, aged 14. She is on the extreme right of the photo, wearing a white blouse.*

▲ *Golda (far right, in a white dress) aged 18 in 1916, when she was teaching at a Yiddish school in the Jewish Centre at Milwaukee.*

She wrote countless letters to Shenya complaining about her situation. Finally, when Golda was fifteen years old, Shenya said she could come and live with her. She and Shamai sent the money for a train ticket and, with Regina Hamburger's help, Golda ran away from home. She did not stay in Denver for long, but the experience gave her her first taste of freedom. Listening to Shenya's friends talking about politics every night made her even more sure of her **Zionist** beliefs. She also fell in love.

Meeting Morris

Morris Meyerson was one of the many friends who visited Shenya and Shamai's home. He was quiet, shy and very studious. He introduced Golda to art, literature and classical music, and gave her books to read. When, just a year later, Golda decided to go home to Milwaukee, Morris told her he wanted to marry her.

Back home

When Golda returned to Milwaukee in 1915, her parents were so happy to have her back that they let her continue at school. There she became even more committed to her political beliefs. As well as campaigning for the Zionist cause, she was a **socialist** and believed in trying to make things better for the poor. She often organized events to raise money for charity. As a woman, she wasn't allowed to speak in the synagogue (the Jewish house of worship), so she stood on a box outside and made impassioned speeches about **socialism** and Zionism. Although her father was annoyed with her for making a spectacle of herself, as a Zionist himself he couldn't help but admire her devotion.

However, Golda's boyfriend Morris did not share her views. He liked his life in the USA and wasn't even very interested in

Zionism. In a move typical of the stubbornness she would show throughout her life, Golda told him she would not compromise. She was going to Palestine with or without him. Unable to bear the thought of losing her, Morris said he would follow her anywhere. So, in 1917, when Golda was just nineteen years old, they married.

◀ *Golda Mabovitch in 1917, the year she married Morris Meyerson.*

5 To Palestine!

In 1917, World War One, which had started in 1914, was near its end. Palestine, which up until then had been ruled by Turkey, was conquered by the British during the war. On 2 November 1917, the British foreign secretary, Arthur Balfour, made a historic statement. He said that Britain was in favour of a Jewish **homeland** being set up in Palestine. This became known as the Balfour Declaration, and **Zionists** around the world welcomed it. Now that they could count on Britain's help, many Jews started preparing to set off for the **Promised Land**. Golda and Morris were among them.

MEDITERRANEAN SEA

SYRIA

IRAQ

•Tel Aviv

Jerusalem•

PALESTINE

TRANSJORDAN

SAUDI ARABIA

BRITISH MANDATE

EGYPT

0   50 km
0   50 miles

N
W—E
S

Area separated and closed to Jewish settlement, 1921

Area ceded to Syria, 1923

Area remaining for Jewish National Homeland

▲ This map shows the lands which were earmarked for Jewish settlement after World War One.

Why did Britain set up a Jewish homeland in Palestine?

In the 19th and early 20th centuries, Britain controlled many parts of the world, such as India, South Africa and Palestine. In those days, British politicians believed they had a right to do whatever they wanted with the lands they ruled, so they saw no problem with giving Palestinian land to the Jews. They also knew that Jews were being attacked and persecuted in many countries, and believed that a Jewish homeland would offer them protection.

Who are the Arabs?

The **Arabs** are a group of people who live in and around the Arabian **peninsula** in the Middle East and across North Africa. They mostly follow the **Muslim** faith and live in countries such as Egypt, Syria, Iraq and Saudi Arabia, as well as Israel. The majority of people living in Palestine were Arabs, and many of them resent the Jews claiming Palestine as their homeland.

Leaving America

They weren't travelling alone: Regina Hamburger, and another friend, Yossel Kopelov, joined them; and then Shenya said she would come with her two children, leaving Shamai to follow

▼ *A street in Tel Aviv in 1921, at the time when Golda, Morris and Shenya arrived in Palestine.*

later. Their families were worried about their safety. The Arab people who lived in Palestine did not welcome the Jewish settlers: there were anti-Jewish riots, and Jews were sometimes killed in Arab attacks. But the decision was made, and on 23 May 1921 the party set off from New York on board the USS *Pocahontas*.

FOR A MAP OF THE PLACES MENTIONED, SEE PAGE 19.

To Tel Aviv

Golda and Morris's journey to Palestine was nightmarish. The crew of their ship **mutinied**, the boat almost sank and the captain took his own life. But the group finally arrived in Italy, and from there took another ship to Egypt and a train to Tel Aviv. Jewish settlers had founded this city in 1909. New buildings were constantly being added, but life there was, to the American newcomers, shockingly basic. There was no grass – the houses stood on scorching desert sand – and many people lived in huts or tents. Even the usually tough Shenya was horrified at the flies crawling all over the food in the market.

Although they soon found an apartment and Golda took a job teaching English, they all felt disappointed. Golda didn't want a teaching job – she wanted to work on the land and help the new nation to feed itself. So she and Morris applied to join a **communal** farm, or **kibbutz**.

Kibbutz life

Golda and Morris were eventually accepted on to Kibbutz Merhavia in the north of Palestine. There they were expected to live communally, doing hard farm work while sharing basic food and sparse living space with 40 other kibbutz members. They also had to learn **Hebrew**, the old Jewish language, which was being revived.

21

Kibbutzim

The first Jewish settlers in Palestine set up communal farms called kibbutzim (the plural of kibbutz) to turn the poor and dry land into productive soil. Kibbutz life was based on the **socialist** ideals of sharing and equality. Inside a kibbutz, everyone had to share the work, space, food and childcare. When the Jewish state of Israel was officially created, the kibbutzim stayed, and many still exist today.

At first, the other kibbutz members thought the Americans would be too soft and spoiled for the kibbutz. But Golda threw herself into her work and grew to love her new way of life. She reared chickens, cleared stones from the soil, planted trees and cooked in the kitchens. She also turned out to be a natural leader and was always being elected on to kibbutz committees. She was even sent to represent Merhavia at conferences where the future of the **Yishuv** (the Jewish settlement in Palestine) was discussed. There, she met the leaders of the Zionist movement, and her interest in politics grew and grew.

Morris's misery

With every day that passed Golda felt happier and more convinced that she was doing the right thing with her life. But for her husband, the opposite was true. Kibbutz life did not suit Morris at all. He liked privacy, books, art and classical music, not shared living spaces and manual labour. He thought the Merhavia members were too serious and didn't appreciate his intelligence and sense of humour. He was not good at farm work, and the hot weather made him ill. He finally said that, if he and Golda were to have children, he didn't want them to

▲ *Jewish women working on a kibbutz in Palestine in the 1920s, as Golda and Morris did after moving there.*

be brought up on a kibbutz. So, in 1924, Golda gave in and did what her husband wanted. She agreed to return to the city.

To Jerusalem

At first, Morris and Golda went back to Tel Aviv to stay with Shenya, but they couldn't find good jobs. Then David Remez, one of the Yishuv leaders Golda had made friends with, offered them jobs in Jerusalem. They were to work for the **Histadrut**, the Jewish labour union, which organized Jewish **immigration** to Palestine, trained the new arrivals and found them jobs.

The day before they left for Jerusalem, Golda discovered that she was pregnant. It seemed like a good omen, and the couple set off for their new lives with hope in their hearts.

The Jerusalem housewife

Golda's baby son, Menachem, was born on 23 November 1924. After his birth, Golda tried to settle into life as a stay-at-home mother and housewife. She caught up with her old friend Regina, who had moved to Jerusalem in 1921, and spent her days shopping and cooking. Although they only had a tiny apartment, with no electricity or running water and a tin shack in the yard for a kitchen, Morris was happy at last. In May 1926, their daughter Sarah was born, and in the same year, Golda's parents moved to Palestine too. Almost her whole family was now in Palestine (only Zipke, who had changed her name to Clara, remained in the USA).

Try as she might, Golda could not settle into a life tied to the home. Although she adored her children, she hated being a housewife. She was desperate to work — not just anywhere, but at the heart of the movement to build a Jewish nation.

A woman's choice

When Menachem was born, Golda realized that there was a conflict in her life. 'I had to decide which came first,' she later wrote, 'my duty to my husband, my home and my child, or the kind of life I myself really wanted.' To begin with she chose duty, but it was not to last.

6 A new job

Golda Meyerson spent four years in Jerusalem trying to make her marriage work, but for her they were unhappy years. She loved Morris, but her personality was so different from his that trying to live the life he wanted made her miserable.

Golda sometimes visited Shenya and her family in Tel Aviv. She also went to see her parents, who lived near Tel Aviv in a town called Herzlia. In 1928, on one of these trips, Golda's old friend David Remez saw her talking to a friend outside the **Histradrut** offices. He went up to her and asked if she would like to return to work – as the secretary of the Histadrut's Women's Labour Council.

The leaders of the Histadrut knew what Golda had to offer. Her passionate commitment to the cause, her natural political ability and her incredible capacity for hard work made her invaluable. But if she took the job it would mean separating from Morris and going to live in Tel Aviv. She said yes.

Separation

Golda knew that her marriage was not working. Reluctantly, she told Morris that they were too different from each other and wanted different things. Although they were to remain friends for the rest of Morris's life, Golda knew she had to put her career first. She took the children, left Morris and moved to Tel Aviv.

Her new job involved training female settlers for **kibbutz** work and organizing jobs for them. She also travelled abroad to tell other Jewish women's organizations about the **Yishuv**. Golda loved the job and threw herself into her new responsibilities, but she felt guilty about being a working mother. At the time, few mothers went out to work, and

Golda's own mother and Shenya often told her that she was neglecting Menachem and Sarah. So she spent every spare second with them, getting up early and staying up late to cook for them, play with them, and take them to clubs, concerts or doctors' appointments. She worried endlessly about whether they were being harmed by her career.

▼ *Jewish people arriving in Haifa, Palestine, in around 1929. As a member of the Histadrut, Golda Meyerson was involved with recruiting such immigrants, and finding them jobs when they arrived.*

New friends

At the Histadrut offices in Tel Aviv, Golda formed close relationships with many of the most powerful people in Jewish Palestine. Her circle was made up of men who, like her, would one day be Israel's leaders. David Ben-Gurion, David Remez, Berl Katznelson, Zalman Shazar and Levi Eshkol were not only great friends, they were also valuable contacts. Knowing them put Golda at the heart of power in the growing Jewish nation.

On her foreign travels too, Golda mixed with politicians and important people from around the world. During trips to the USA and Britain, she sensed a lot of support for the Jewish settlers. She hoped that she could help to achieve what she had always dreamed of, and turn the Yishuv – the Jewish settlement – into a proper country.

Key dates: marriage, motherhood and career

1917	• December	Marriage to Morris Meyerson
1921	• July	The Meyersons arrive in Palestine
1921	• October	They start living at Merhavia Kibbutz
1924	• February	They move to Tel Aviv, then to Jerusalem to start a family
1924	• November	Birth of their son Menachem
1926	• May	Birth of their daughter Sarah
1928		Morris and Golda separate, and Golda moves to Tel Aviv to start her new job with the Histadrut

To America

In 1932, Sarah fell very ill with kidney disease. Morris and Golda were afraid that the hospitals in Palestine would not be able to help her. So Golda arranged to visit the USA on behalf of the Histadrut, to raise money and support for the Yishuv. She took the children with her and, in hospital in New York, Sarah made a good recovery. For once, Golda's career and her children's needs were not in conflict.

They were to stay in the USA for two years. Golda's work there was a huge success. She was brilliant at campaigning, public speaking and raising money for the Jewish cause, and found fame as an international representative of Jewish Palestine.

On her return to Palestine in 1934, she was elected to the **Va'ad Hapoel**, the **executive committee** of the Histadrut. In effect, this made her one of the leaders of the Yishuv. Jewish Palestine had no other government except its faraway British rulers, and the Va'ad Hapoel had gradually grown into a kind of ruling body. For the next fifteen years, Golda would use this position to work towards making the Yishuv – or Israel, as it would come to be known – into an independent state.

People and politics

The Yishuv was a Jewish name for the large group of Jews who had settled in Palestine. Although they were not a proper state yet, they tried to live together like a nation. The Histadrut started off as the labour union of the Yishuv, but it gradually turned into a kind of ruling political party. Va'ad Hapoel was the committee of politicians who controlled the Histadrut, and so controlled the Yishuv.

7 Problems for Palestine

In the mid-1930s, Palestine was still controlled by the British. As long ago as 1917, the British government had said it was in favour of a Jewish **homeland** being founded there – but would it stick to its word? Britain's role in Palestine was about to be put to a terrible test.

FOR DETAILS ON KEY PEOPLE OF MEIR'S TIME, SEE PAGE 58.

In Germany, Adolf Hitler, leader of the **Nazi Party**, was in power. He blamed the Jews for Germany's problems and for its defeat in World War One. Once in power Hitler's hatred of the Jews became very evident. He began to turn against Jews and other **minorities**, creating laws and promoting ideas that **discriminated** against them. Jewish people started to flee from Germany – and where better to go than their **Promised Land**? As the 1930s progressed, increasing numbers of Jews began to arrive in Palestine. The **Histadrut** welcomed them, but the British were not happy, and tried to discourage Jewish **immigration** because they were now worried about fighting breaking out between **Arabs** and Jews in Palestine.

▶ *A woman reads an anti-Jewish poster displayed in a shop window in Germany in 1933.*

The rise of Hitler

Initially Hitler's Nazi Party promised to improve life for all Germans. They certainly improved the German economy, which had suffered following World War One. But the Nazi Party also supported the idea that some humans were better than others. Jews, black people, gypsies and the disabled were treated as sub-humans. Nonetheless, the party was popular with many German people, and rapidly gained power during the 1930s.

A plan for two states

Britain's main concern was that Arabs who lived in and around Palestine would object to more Jewish settlers. There were already riots, and Jewish settlers were still being killed in attacks by Arabs. In response, an underground Jewish fighting force, the **Haganah**, had formed. Palestinian Jews disagreed with one other about what to do. Golda Meyerson, and many others on **Va'ad Hapoel**, favoured self-restraint ('havlaga') – in other words they opposed making the violence worse. Those on the **right wing** believed in answering the Arab attacks with violence.

In 1937, Britain came up with a plan for creating two separate states in Palestine, one for Arabs and one for Jews. But no one could agree about the plan, and nothing came of it. The future of Palestine was still unclear.

The White Paper and war

In the late 1930s, Hitler's armies started to invade large areas of Europe. In the countries occupied by Germany – including Austria and Czechoslovakia – Jews were driven from their homes and had their businesses and jobs taken away. More and more refugees queued up to enter Palestine. But the British, afraid of upsetting the Arabs, decided to stop Jewish immigration. In May 1939, they released a **White Paper** (a government document) proposing the restriction of new arrivals to 15,000 Jews per year. After five years, the document said, Jewish immigration should stop altogether.

Golda and the other **Yishuv** leaders were furious. Now the Jews had three fronts to deal with – Hitler's Nazi regime, the Arab groups that were attacking settlers, and the British

▲ *When the British 1939 White Paper restricted Jewish immigration to Palestine, Jews protested against it in the streets of Jerusalem.*

government's stand on the White Paper – all of which were threatening their dream of a homeland open to all Jews.

In September 1939, Britain and France finally declared war on Germany, and World War Two began. The Histadrut were ready for battle too. As soon as they could, they intended to win complete independence for Israel.

8 War and horror

World War Two continued for more than six years, and it was a time of terrible frustration for Golda. She desperately wanted the **Yishuv** to help the Jews who were being **persecuted** in Europe. But Britain was blocking Jewish **immigration** from Nazi-occupied Europe, sending its soldiers to guard the Palestinian coast and preventing Jewish refugee ships from leaving Europe. At the beginning of the war, however, Golda had no idea what was really happening to Jews and other **minorities** in German territory. It was not just **discrimination**: it was much, much worse.

Illegal immigration

The **Histadrut** believed that, to show support for European Jews, it would be justified in helping them to enter Palestine illegally. Golda was closely involved with **underground** attempts to smuggle Jews into Jewish areas of Palestine, out of sight of British officials.

Unsurprisingly, there was little trust between British and Jewish leaders. On one occasion, members of the **Haganah** were accused of stealing the British army's weapons. Golda Meyerson was called to give evidence in the case, and amazed the court with her sarcastic replies to the British lawyer. She

Key dates: world at war		
1933	• January	Adolf Hitler comes to power in Germany
1939	• September	World War Two begins
1939–1945	• Millions of Jews die in the Holocaust	
1945	• September	End of World War Two
1948	• May 14	Israel declares its independence

▲ *During World War Two, Arabs and Jews living in Palestine volunteered to fight for the British. Here they are marching side by side during a training exercise in 1940.*

defended the rights of all Jews to arm themselves against attack, wherever their weapons might come from. Her performance greatly impressed the Yishuv leaders.

Jewish fighters

Despite all this, the Yishuv was still governed by Britain, and large numbers of Palestinian Jews fought for the **Allies** during the war. The Histadrut was deeply opposed to Hitler and his regime, and its members hoped that Britain would reward the Jews for their efforts by granting them independence when the war was over.

In 1943, the Histadrut even persuaded Britain to let it parachute-drop 42 Jewish soldiers (mainly Haganah volunteers) behind enemy lines. The aim was to free Allied prisoners and support Jews who were opposing Hitler. Although they had some success, most of the volunteers were killed in the exercise, and Golda lost several close friends.

The Holocaust

As the war went on, rumours about what was happening inside Europe began to reach Palestine. Jewish people who had escaped reported that the Nazis were rounding up Jews and taking them to prison camps, where they were tortured, killed or used in horrific medical experiments. When the Jewish leaders first heard these stories, they decided to send investigators to try to find out more. Golda happened to

▼ 7 May 1945: emaciated prisoners at Ebensee concentration camp in Austria at the end of World War Two.

mention this to a British official she was friendly with. He was amazed that she took the rumours seriously. 'You mustn't believe everything you hear,' he told her kindly.

It was all true, however. The Nazis were eventually defeated, and as the war drew to its close in 1944 and 1945, the full horror of what had been happening to the Jews was discovered. Huge numbers of those who had not managed to escape from German-occupied territories had been herded into concentration camps such as Auschwitz and Treblinka. There they had been starved, tortured, executed in purpose-built gas chambers and dumped in mass graves. Altogether, more than six million Jews and members of other minorities were murdered in this terrible **genocide**, which became known as the **Holocaust**.

After the war, the Jews were sure their time had come. They had suffered enough – surely the British would now allow the surviving Jewish refugees to come to Palestine. But the opposite was the case. The British government clamped down on the Histadrut, arresting many of its leaders for their disobedience during the war. Now it was time to fight for freedom.

The concentration camps

During World War Two there were dozens of Nazi concentration camps, mainly in Germany, Austria and Poland. At first, prisoners were just used for labour, but soon the Nazis set up death camps specifically designed to wipe out as many Jews and other **minorities** as possible. Many who did survive had almost starved to death by the time they were rescued at the end of the war.

9 Israel is born!

In June 1946 Britain wanted to control the **Yishuv** and stop **immigration**. Many **Va'ad Hapoel** members were arrested (their leader, David Ben-Gurion, went abroad to avoid arrest). Golda Meyerson, however, was not arrested. Perhaps because she was a woman the British did not think she posed a problem. Or perhaps they didn't want to anger the Jewish public by detaining one of the Yishuv's most popular politicians. Either way, in 1946 Golda found herself acting head of Va'ad Hapoel, and unofficial leader of the Yishuv.

FOR DETAILS ON KEY PEOPLE OF MEIR'S TIME, SEE PAGE 58.

Peaceful protests

Many Jews in Palestine were prepared to fight the British with weapons. Members of the **Haganah** went into hiding and launched attacks on British officers. But Golda lived in hope of a peaceful solution. Instead of military attacks, she organized

▼ *Many Jews who had escaped from the concentration camps wanted to move to Israel, but ended up being put in prison on the island of Cyprus by the British in 1946. Here a group of them are protesting with a sign that reads: 'From lager (prison camp) to lager — till when?'*

► *Women taking an oath as they become members of the Haganah, the Jewish secret army, in Tel Aviv, Israel, in 1948.*

street protests and civil disobedience against the British. The latter involved peacefully refusing to obey British laws – a tactic that was also being used against British control in India.

On one occasion, Golda even took part in a hunger strike. The British were refusing to allow two ships filled with Jewish refugees to sail to Palestine from Italy. The refugees went on hunger strike, and Golda persuaded the Yishuv leaders to join them. They went without food for days until the ships were allowed to set off.

Crack down

Still the British did not give in to the Jews' demands for a **homeland**. Instead, in 1947, they started to arrest illegal Jewish immigrants and took them to offshore prison camps, for example, on the island of Cyprus. The Jews were furious, and the violence and civil disobedience escalated. The situation was becoming impossible.

Finally, the **United Nations** (UN), an international organization formed just after the war, stepped in. It set up a committee to debate the situation in Palestine and to vote on its future. On 29 November 1947, the committee voted in favour of the separation of Palestine into a Jewish state and an Arab state. This was accepted by the Jews but not the **Arabs**.

War worries

The Yishuv leaders, now free from prison, were delighted with the UN vote. But they knew that if they were granted independence, the Arab countries in the area would be angry. The new Jewish state would probably have to fight its neighbours to establish its borders, and to do so it needed support from abroad.

David Ben-Gurion was poised to become the leader of the new state. He was planning to visit the USA to ask for help, but Golda pointed out that he was needed to lead the Jews at home. So, in January 1948, the Va'ad Hapoel members voted that Golda should go instead. She had proved herself a brilliant fundraiser, she had friends in the USA and spoke fluent English. She set off immediately.

David Ben-Gurion

Born in Plonsk, Poland in 1886, David Ben-Gurion was a lifelong **Zionist**. He arrived in Palestine in 1906 and was involved in the early **kibbutz** movement and with the **Histadrut**. As leader of the Histadrut and the Mapai Party, he became Israel's first prime minister in 1948 and held the post twice before retiring in 1963. Nicknamed 'the Old Man' in later life, he finally died in 1973, aged 87.

Golda's missions

In the USA Golda Meyerson raised an astonishing 50 million dollars for the new Jewish state. Americans – especially American Jews – responded in their thousands to her powerful and emotive speeches. Without this massive contribution it would have been impossible to set up the new country. On her return, Golda undertook more missions –

some of which were secret and highly dangerous. She went to visit Abdullah, king of Jordan, one of the Arab countries closest to the Yishuv, in an attempt to negotiate peace with the Arabs.

A declaration of independence

In spring 1948, David Ben-Gurion was ready to declare independence. All the Jewish leaders knew it was a risk. The British would not support them, and they would probably have to fight several Arab nations at once. But with support, money and arms from the USA, they thought they had a chance. So, on 14 May 1948, the new state of Israel was officially proclaimed at a ceremony in Tel Aviv. As leader of **Mapai**, Israel's leading political party, Ben-Gurion became the country's first prime minister.

▲ David Ben-Gurion, prime minister of the new state of Israel (centre right, with jacket), watches the final withdrawal of the British government from Israel at Haifa in July 1948.

Golda remembered the independence ceremony as an emotional occasion. 'The State of Israel!' she later wrote in her autobiography. 'My eyes filled with tears, and my hands shook. We had done it! We had brought the Jewish state into existence – and I, Golda Mabovitch Meyerson, had lived to see the day.'

The USA recognized the new state almost immediately. But there was trouble ahead. The very next day, Israel was under attack from six of its Arab neighbours: Jordan, Egypt, Saudi Arabia, Syria, Lebanon and Iraq. The war of independence had begun.

The new state of Israel, just a few days old, was under siege. Jerusalem was a battleground; the road between Jerusalem and Tel Aviv was lined with **snipers**; and war raged along Israel's new borders. But Golda Meyerson was sure that Israel would win its battle to exist. She wanted to be where the action was, and hoped for a place in the new Israeli **Cabinet**. During a visit to the USA in June 1948, however, she heard that she had been appointed the Israeli **ambassador** to Moscow.

This was an important job, but Golda was disappointed. It meant that she would be isolated from her colleagues and unable to help with the war effort. Nevertheless she responded to the call of duty – despite having broken her leg in a taxi crash before leaving the USA. By September 1948, she was in Moscow.

Winning the war

Although Golda could not be there, the money and support she had raised helped Israel's war effort, and it finally won the war of independence in January 1949. Negotiations took place to draw up border agreements and peace treaties. There was also an election, and Ben-Gurion was returned to power. He appointed Golda Meyerson as minister of labour in his Cabinet. She was recalled from Moscow.

◀ *Prime Minister David Ben-Gurion and foreign minister Golda Meir at a meeting with the leader of the* **United Nations**, *Dag Hammarskjoeld (far right), in 1957.*

The duties of minister of labour were similar to those that Golda had undertaken for the **Histadrut** twenty years earlier. They included organizing jobs, homes and training for thousands of Jewish immigrants, whom Israel was now able to welcome with open arms. Golda also went on many more fundraising trips to Europe and the USA.

Foreign minister

Golda performed so well, especially on her trips abroad, that Israel's leaders began to realize she was worthy of an even more important job. In 1956, she was appointed foreign minister – a position second in command only to Ben-Gurion. However, there was another reason for the appointment. Ben-Gurion wanted to rid himself of Moshe Sharrett, the previous foreign minister and prime minister. While Ben-Gurion wanted to take an aggressive stance towards the **Arab** states, the more liberal Sharrett was in favour of reconciliation and the use of diplomacy. Golda was keen on diplomacy too, but Ben-Gurion thought she would be less trouble than Sharrett. Golda not only had to deal with the responsibilities of her new job, she also had to cope with her old friend Sharrett's anger at being pushed to one side.

FOR DETAILS ON KEY PEOPLE OF MEIR'S TIME, SEE PAGE 58.

The war of independence

Israel's war of independence began on 15 May 1948 when six Arab countries – Egypt, Syria, Jordan, Iraq, Saudi Arabia and Lebanon – attacked their new neighbour. The Arab armies had more fighters and more equipment, but communication between the countries was poor. Although it was outnumbered, Israel's army was very well organized and trained. The fighting took place in small bursts, with ceasefires in between, until Israel had taken over more land than it had to start with. In January 1949 the war officially ended, but many Arab states remained hostile towards Israel.

At this time, Golda changed her last name from Meyerson to Meir. Senior members of the government were expected to have **Hebrew** names, to reflect Israel's policy of using Hebrew as its official language. Golda picked the name Meir, meaning 'illuminate', partly because it resembled her old name.

Big responsibilities

Throughout her life Golda Meir proved more than capable of doing any job that was handed to her. The role of foreign minister was hard work, especially dealing with disagreements inside the government as well as international tensions. But Golda succeeded, drawing on all her courage, **charisma** and **diplomatic** skill. She travelled the world, representing the new state on visits to dozens of countries, conferences and committees.

Suez

The Suez Crisis occurred because President Nasser of Egypt was angry with the British and French for withdrawing the money he needed to build Egypt's Aswan Dam. Nasser wanted an independent Egypt and thought he could achieve this by aligning himself with the Soviet Union rather than the USA. By seizing control of the Suez Canal, he denied the Europeans a vital trading route to India and the rest of Asia. Israel also needed the Suez Canal, and the nearby Straits of Tiran, for sea access to Israel's southernmost tip at Eilat.

In July 1956, during Golda Meir's term as foreign minister, the Suez Crisis occurred. This was a dispute over the control of the Suez Canal, which links the Mediterranean and Red seas. The canal had previously been owned by the Suez Canal Company, in which Britain had nearly half the share. Egypt's president, Gamal Abdel-Nasser,

nationalized the canal, and Britain and France secretly joined forces with Israel to try to seize it back. The Israeli army was successful and took over a large area of Egyptian territory, but the United Nations ordered that it be handed back. A compromise was reached, but Golda felt let down by the UN and by her old friend, the USA. She spent much of the rest of her time as foreign minister rebuilding Israel's relationship with the USA. She also visited Africa and developed good friendships with many of the countries there.

Personal problems

Although her career was at its highest point yet, this was a difficult time in Golda's private life. In 1951, her estranged husband Morris died. He was staying at her home in Jerusalem at the time, but typically she was away on work business. Her mother died the same year; her daughter Sarah became unwell again; and Golda herself was not in good health. By 1965, she was so exhausted that she decided to retire as foreign minister and spend more time being a good mother and grandmother, although she did remain as general secretary of her party. Little did she know that the pinnacle of her career was yet to come.

FOR DETAILS ON KEY PEOPLE OF MEIR'S TIME, SEE PAGE 58.

▼ *The people of Port Said in Egypt wander the streets after an attack by British and French troops during the Suez Crisis.*

Israel won the first war against its **Arab** neighbours in 1949, but its problems were far from over. Arab groups in and around Palestine still launched attacks against Israeli citizens, and Israel's leaders argued fiercely with one another about what to do in response. Meanwhile, the Arab nations still planned to take back land now in Israel, which they saw as theirs by right. When Golda Meir retired as foreign minister in 1965, the state of no war and no peace continued. Several Arab states prepared themselves for another war against Israel.

▼ *In a rare moment of relaxation, Foreign Minister Golda Meir plays with her grandchildren in Israel in 1961.*

A new prime minister

Prime Minister Ben-Gurion retired in 1963 and Levi Eshkol was chosen to replace him as head of the **Mapai Party**. Golda was secretary-general of Mapai. But soon after Eshkol took over the leadership, Ben-Gurion and Eshkol fell out.

FOR DETAILS ON KEY PEOPLE OF MEIR'S TIME, SEE PAGE 58.

Power behind the throne

Although she had retired as foreign minister, Golda Meir still played an important role in Israeli politics. As secretary-general of the Mapai Party, she found that government leaders came to her for advice on international issues, and reported on progress not to the prime minister, but to her. Even Eshkol asked her advice.

More war on the way

In May 1967, Egypt again closed off the Straits of Tiran, the southern sea route vital to Israel. This was essentially a declaration of war. Israel would have to fight Egypt to win control of the straits, and other Arab states were poised to join in. Egypt, Syria and Jordan were all massing weapons and fighter planes on Israel's borders, ready for battle.

The Israeli people wanted Eshkol to attack Egypt immediately. When he failed to do so, there were calls for the appointment of the former head of the Israel defence forces, Moshe Dayan, as defence minister. Golda did not want this. She wanted a peaceful solution and would have preferred to negotiate with the Arabs. But she was confident that Israel had the power to win the coming war. Eventually, the government bowed to public pressure and, at the beginning of June 1967, Dayan became defence minister. As expected, he went to work. On 5 June, he launched lightning strikes on Arab airbases to destroy their waiting aircraft before they could take off. Israel was at war again.

▲ *An Egyptian fighter plane, destroyed by Israeli forces during the Six-Day War in 1967, lies wrecked on the ground at El Arish, Egypt.*

The Six-Day War

This war lasted just six days, from 5–10 June 1967, and became one of the most famous in Israel's short and battle-filled history. The unexpected Israeli strikes made all the difference – the Arabs were weakened and unable to launch the attacks they had planned. The Israelis' aggressive action not only protected their interests, it also enabled them to take over new lands more than three times the size of their existing territory. More than a million Arabs living in these areas were now under Israeli control. Parts of Jerusalem that had previously been controlled by the Arabs were opened to the Jews again, including the Western Wall, an ancient Jewish holy site.

The whole country united in rejoicing, and Dayan was hailed as a hero. Meanwhile, Golda Meir focused on a new task. The Mapai Party had been so divided over the war that it had split into two separate groups. Through many meetings and negotiations, Meir managed to create a new party – the **Labour Party**.

Meir now decided that it really was time to take a back seat. She stepped down as secretary-general in July 1968, and prepared to spend more time with her family and friends.

Too much for Eshkol

Throughout this time, Prime Minister Eshkol had been unwell, and he died on 26 February 1969. Following the success of the Six-Day War, Moshe Dayan was popular with the public, and could have easily stepped into Eshkol's shoes. But many in the newly formed Labour Party did not want such a hard-line politician and a member of the younger generation at the top. They wanted a wise, moderate leader who could hold the party together until things had calmed down. Soon after Eshkol's death, many members of the party begged Golda Meir to take over – just until public elections could be held in October.

Although Golda had tried on numerous occasions to retire, the lure of politics always called her back. She was unwell – she had been diagnosed with cancer – yet the needs of her country meant everything to her. She consulted with her children and her nephew Yonah, Shenya's son, who all said she should take the job. Finally, she was ready to accept the leadership. The Labour Party members held a vote and Golda Meir was **unanimously** elected party leader. She became prime minister of Israel on 7 March 1969.

On becoming prime minister

When she was voted in as prime minister, Golda Meir later said, she was in shock. 'I know that tears rolled down my cheeks and that I held my head in my hands when the voting was over... ' she recalled. 'I was dazed. I had never planned to be prime minister.'

Leading Israel in 1969 was not an easy task. Terrorist attacks were still commonplace – in the very week that Golda Meir took office, a bomb exploded in a student café in Jerusalem, injuring 29 people. Meir often found herself attending funerals for victims of **terrorism**. And, although this was a time of relative peace, Israel's armies were constantly occupied with defending the borders of the huge new territories they had taken over in the Six-Day War.

American support

One of Golda Meir's first actions as prime minister was her famous state visit to the USA (mentioned on pages 4–5). Although US President Richard Nixon had been reluctant to help Israel with more weapons and money, when he met with Golda face-to-face she managed to persuade him to sell her country modern fighting equipment. She also made public speeches and held **press conferences**, and her popularity with the American public seemed to be greater than ever.

Israel had the military power to succeed in war largely because of Golda's good relationship with the USA, and for this the Israeli public rated her highly. Previously, everyone had expected Moshe Dayan or another contender, Yigal Allon, to win the Israeli elections in October 1969. But by the time the elections were held, Israelis no longer saw Golda Meir as a stand-in. She was elected with a huge majority.

▶ *Election posters featuring Golda Meir on display in Jerusalem during the Israeli elections in October 1969.*

Life at the top

At 71 years of age, Golda Meir now found herself with a busier schedule than ever before. The long hours and her poor health left her exhausted, and she often slept during the day after working late into the night. Her eyesight was failing,

▲ *The new prime minister gives a speech at a Labour Party Conference in Tel Aviv in 1970.*

so she relied heavily on her two close aides, Lou Kaddar and Simcha Dinitz, to read her important **telegrams** every evening. They also had to organize her diary, fitting in all her public appointments while still allowing time to spend with her family. Once, when she wanted to meet her younger sister Clara at the airport but was booked up with work, the stress was too much for her and she hurled an ashtray across the room. She later apologized, but her aides learned not to make the same mistake again.

The Kitchen Cabinet

As always, Meir mixed work with home life. On every Monday there was a formal **Cabinet** meeting, so on Sunday nights she would invite her party colleagues to her house to discuss policy. These informal meetings became known as 'Golda's Kitchen Cabinet'. She even took on the role of a traditional Jewish grandmother, making chicken soup for her younger male colleagues. Yet no one underestimated her: she was always in control.

Peace and prosperity

With Golda Meir's influence, there was financial and military support from the Americans. The government was able to focus on non-military issues, such as improving housing and employment opportunities for Israelis and developing the tourist industry.

Golda also hoped to begin peace talks with the **Arab** states – especially Egypt and Jordan. She had always believed that it would be better to negotiate with the Arabs rather than fight wars with them. She held secret talks with King Hussein of Jordan. But Hussein wanted Israel to return all the land it had taken in 1967, and the two leaders could not agree. Meanwhile, the **Palestine Liberation Organization** was gaining in strength under a new leader, Yasser Arafat.

Nonetheless, Israel felt good about itself. It had international support and its borders were strong. As Yitzhak Rabin, who would one day be prime minister himself, put it: 'Golda Meir has better boundaries than King David or King Solomon.' So, when war broke out again in 1973, it came as a surprise.

The Yom Kippur War

This war broke out on Yom Kippur, one of the holiest days in the Jewish calendar. In 1973, Yom Kippur fell on Saturday, 6 October. There was a slight air of tension in Israel – military leaders had warned that armies were gathering in Syria. But most people agreed that Syria was not planning to attack.

However, at 4 a.m. on the day before Yom Kippur, the Israeli military received a warning that Egypt and Syria would declare war the next day at 6 p.m. When Golda heard the news, she knew she had to mobilize forces in both north and south

▲ *Golda Meir inspects a guard of honour at Tel Aviv in October 1970, just before leaving for a meeting of the* **United Nations** *in New York.*

Israel. Despite the warning, she did not want Israel to attack first because this would make the Israelis appear aggressive, and that might make the USA withdraw its support. Eventually, attacks were launched at around 1p.m. on 6 October, and there were heavy Israeli losses. But Golda would not give in. She managed to obtain help from the USA once again, and Israel finally beat back the attack. A ceasefire was declared on 25 October.

Time to go

When elections were held late in 1973, the **Labour Party** was voted back in and Golda Meir won support from her colleagues to continue as prime minister. However, many people wanted to know why she had not seen the Yom Kippur War coming, and why more than 2500 young Israeli soldiers had lost their lives. Although it was decided at an inquiry that she had acted properly throughout, Golda was racked with guilt. She was also old, tired and still battling cancer. It was time to retire.

After forming a new Cabinet, Golda Meir formally resigned from her prime ministerial post and from her seat in the **Knesset** (the Israeli parliament) on 10 April 1974.

▲ *Prime Minister Meir meets with newly arrived Jewish immigrants from Russia in Jerusalem in June 1971.*

Meir in power

1963	• June	David Ben-Gurion resigns as prime minister, appointing Levi Eshkol in his place
1969	• February	Eshkol dies and Golda Meir takes his place a few days later as prime minister
1969	• September	Meir visits the USA to raise support for Israel
1973	• October	Many Israelis die in the Yom Kippur War
1974	• April	Golda Meir resigns as prime minister

13 Golda Meir's legacy

In 1978, just four years after stepping down as prime minister, Golda Meir died in Jerusalem at the age of 80, of the cancer she had fought for fifteen years. She had spent her retirement, as ever, in demand – writing her autobiography *My Life*, travelling widely, and staying active in politics as an adviser to her former colleagues. At the time of her death, she was renowned and admired throughout the world as a wise, tough and unique politician. But what did she leave behind?

Peace in Israel?

All her life, Golda had longed for a Jewish **homeland** where her people could live in peace. She wanted Jews to live in harmony with their **Arab** neighbours, and indeed with all other peoples and cultures. But when it came to defending Israel, she was prepared to fight. She believed deeply that Israel had a right to exist, and that if Israelis were attacked, they had a right to defend themselves.

▼ *Still busy after her retirement: Golda Meir laughs during a meeting with the new US president Gerald Ford at the White House in 1975.*

▲ *Friends and supporters follow Golda Meir's coffin at her state funeral in Jerusalem in December 1978.*

In the end, peace was not achieved in the Middle East during Golda Meir's lifetime. In that sense, she did not achieve her aims. Because like many of the older generation, she did not recognize the importance of the Palestinians. She once said: 'There is no such thing as a Palestinian.' However, she did play a major role in creating the state of Israel. Her hard work at the **Histadrut**, her devotion to the struggle against the

British, and most of all her amazing ability to raise funds and support from abroad were all vital to the survival of the infant Jewish state in its first few years.

A woman's work

Perhaps equally importantly, Golda Meir played a huge part in breaking down the barriers that prevented women from achieving political power. She showed that if someone was the best person for a job, it didn't matter whether that person was male or female.

When she was asked whether she was a **feminist**, however, she often said she didn't agree with feminism if it involved hating men or not having children. She had always taken her role as a wife and mother seriously, and worried about neglecting it for her career. Although she was regarded as a hero by many, she never really promoted feminism for its own sake. She didn't think that women were better than men, but simply that everyone had to pull together. Since her time at the Kibbutz Merhavia, when everyone took an equal share of the work, she never saw why being a woman should make any difference. She wanted to be remembered not necessarily as a woman, but as a politician.

Goodbye Golda

Golda Meir's obituary in the *New York Times* on 9 December 1978 concluded: 'At the end of her life she was still feeling guilty about the years during which she had neglected her children and about her failure to devote herself to the **kibbutz** rather than to public life. "There is a type of woman who cannot remain at home," she once wrote. "In spite of the place her children and family fill in her life, her nature demands something more; she cannot divorce herself from the larger social life. She cannot let her children narrow her horizon. For such a woman, there is no rest." '

Timeline

1898	Golda Mabovitch is born on 3 May in Kiev, Russia, the second of three sisters.
1903	Golda's father, Moshe Mabovitch, goes to the USA to find work.
1905	The rest of family join Moshe in Milwaukee, Wisconsin, USA.
1913	Golda runs away to Denver, Colorado, to live with her sister Shenya.
1914	Golda returns to Milkwaukee and continues her education.
1917	At the age of nineteen, Golda marries Morris Meyerson in Milwaukee. The Balfour Declaration states that Britain is in favour of a Jewish **homeland** being founded in Palestine.
1921	Golda and Morris move to Palestine. They join **Kibbutz** Merhavia.
1924	Golda and Morris move back to Tel Aviv. They then move to Jerusalem to work for the **Histadrut** (national labour union). In November their first child Menachem (meaning 'comfort') is born and Golda gives up work.
1926	Their second child, Sarah, is born in May.
1928	Golda and Morris separate and Golda moves to Tel Aviv with her children to take up a new job with the Women's Labour Council of the Histadrut.
1932	Sarah becomes seriously ill and Golda takes her children to the USA, where Sarah recovers in hospital. Golda works as a campaigner and fundraiser for the **Yishuv** (Jewish settlement of Palestine).
1933	Adolf Hitler comes to power in Germany.
1930s	Jewish **immigration** to Palestine increases as European Jews flee German territories.
1939	A British **White Paper** restricts Jewish immigration to Palestine.
1939	World War Two breaks out.
1944	The full extent of the **Holocaust** (mass murder of European Jews) begins to be revealed.

1945	End of World War Two.
1946	Golda Meyerson acts as temporary leader of the Histadrut after most of her colleagues are arrested by the British.
1947	The **United Nations** votes in favour of an independent Jewish state being founded in Palestine,
1948	Golda Meyerson travels to the USA and raises $50 million for the Israel independence effort. The new state of Israel declares independence (14 May) and David Ben-Gurion, leader of the dominant **Mapai Party**, becomes its first prime minister. Golda Meyerson becomes Israel's **ambassador** to Moscow.
1949	Israel wins the war of independence against its Arab neighbours. Golda Meyerson is called back from Moscow and becomes minister for labour.
1956	Golda Meyerson becomes Israeli foreign minister. Golda Meyerson changes her name to Golda Meir.
1956	The Suez Crisis erupts over control of the Suez Canal.
1957	Foreign Minister Meir begins a series of visits to Africa and Asia.
1963	David Ben-Gurion resigns as prime minister and appoints Levi Eshkol in his place.
1965	Golda Meir resigns as foreign minister.
1967	Israel captures large areas of Arab land in the Six-Day War.
1969	Golda Meir resigns as secretary-general of the **Labour** (formerly Mapai) **Party**. Levi Eshkol dies (February) and Golda Meir is appointed temporary prime minister (March). Meir undertakes a US state visit and tour (September). The Israelis elect Golda Meir as prime minister (October).
1973	Israel suffers heavy losses in the Yom Kippur War in October. The Labour Party is re-elected with Golda Meir as prime minister.
1974	Golda Meir resigns as prime minister.
1978	Golda Meir dies in Jerusalem on 8 December, aged 80.

Key people of Golda Meir's time

Ben-Gurion, David (1886–1973). Leading **Zionist**. Born in Poland, he moved to Palestine in 1909. He was a founder member of the **kibbutz** movement and of the **Histadrut**, the Jewish national labour union. As head of the **Mapai Party**, he led the struggle to establish Israel as an independent state, and became its first prime minister after independence was declared in May 1948. After a short break in the mid-1950s, he returned to power and finally resigned as Israeli leader in 1963. He died in 1973, aged 87.

Eshkol, Levi (1895–1969). Israel's prime minister from 1963 to 1969, Eshkol was born in Kiev, Russia and moved to Palestine in 1914. He worked as a Zionist campaigner and farmer, and joined the **Haganah** (**underground** army) in 1940. After Israel became independent, he served as agriculture minister and finance minister before being installed as prime minister in 1963. He died while still in office in 1969, at the age of 73.

Herzl, Theodor (1860–1904). A founder of modern **Zionism** (the belief in a Jewish homeland), Herzl was born in Hungary and worked as a journalist in Paris. He spread Zionism through his conferences and publications and founded the World Zionist Organization in 1897. In 1904 he died at the young age of 44, long before the state of Israel came into being.

Hitler, Adolf (1889–1945). Founder and leader of the German **Nazi Party**, which came to power in Germany in 1933. He presided over the **persecution** and murder of six million Jews and the killing of many other **minority** groups. His invasion of lands around Germany led to the outbreak of World War Two in 1939.

King Hussein of Jordan (1935–1999). Leader of Jordan, Israel's neighbour and, after 1994, closest friend in the Arab world. Hussein's grandfather, King Abdullah, was assassinated in 1951. After his father, King Talal, resigned because of ill health, Hussein became king in 1952, aged just sixteen. He was renowned for his attempts to negotiate peace in the Middle East. He died in 1999.

Abdel-Nasser, Gamal (1918–1970). Egypt's president from 1954–1970, Nasser rose from a poor background to lead his country. His **nationalization** of the Suez Canal in 1956 led to the Suez Crisis, involving Israel, Britain and France, and he was instrumental in starting the Six-Day War against Israel in 1967. He died of a heart attack while still in office.

Nixon, Richard (1913–1994). US president from 1969–1974, at the same time as Golda Meir was Israel's leader. Nixon gave Israel much-needed financial and military support after Golda Meir's state visit to the USA in 1969. He was forced to resign from office after the **Watergate scandal** in 1974.

Sadat, Anwar (1918–1981). Egyptian leader from 1970 to 1981, Sadat led Egypt into the Yom Kippur War with Israel in 1973. He later negotiated a peace deal with Israeli leader Menachem Begin, for which they shared the Nobel Peace Prize in 1978. He was assassinated in 1981 by **Muslim** extremists who were opposed to the deal.

Places to visit and further reading

Places to visit

Golda Meir House and Museum, 1146 Ninth Street Park, Auraria Campus, Denver, Colorado, USA: Golda Meir's home in Denver

Golda Meir's grave on top of Mount Herzl, outside Jerusalem

Websites

Heinemann Explore, an online resource for Key Stage 3 history:
  www.heinemannexplore.co.uk
United States Holocaust Memorial Museum:
  www.ushmm.org
Guardian Unlimited History of the Arab-Israeli conflict:
  www.guardian.co.uk/wto/flash/0,6189,380127,00.html
Quotations by Women: Golda Meir:
  womenshistory.about.com/library/qu/blqumeir.htm
New York Times obituary of Golda Meir:
  www.nytimes.com/learning/general/onthisday/bday/0503.html

Further reading

Our Golda: The Story of Golda Meir, David A. Adler, The Viking Press, 1984

A Life For Israel: The Story of Golda Meir, Arnold Dobrin, The Dial Press, 1974

Golda Meir (The Importance of series), Deborah Hitzeroth, Greenhaven Press, 1997

Golda Meir, Karen McAuley, Chambers, 1991

Sources

My Life, Golda Meir, G. P. Putnam's Sons, 1975

Golda: The Uncrowned Queen of Israel, Robert Slater, Jonathan David Publishers, 1981

Golda: The Life of Israel's Prime Minister, Peggy Mann, Pocket Books, 1973

Glossary

Allies, the consisted of Britain, the USA, France, Australia, New Zealand and the Soviet Union, who fought together in World War Two against the Axis powers (Germany, Italy and Japan)

ambassador politician sent to represent a country abroad

Arabs group of peoples from countries in the Middle East and North Africa

Cabinet senior members of a government

charisma magnetic personal presence

communal shared between a group of people

cossack soldier who served the Tsar in pre-1917 Russia

diaspora widespread distribution of peoples around the world. Often used to describe the movements of Jews following the conquest of Jerusalem and the destruction of the Jewish temple by the Romans more than 2000 years ago

diplomatic concerning relations between the governments of different countries

discrimination unfavourable treatment based on prejudice, especially because of race, religion or gender

ethnic concerning the race or culture of a group of people

ethnic minority group of people who share the same culture, race or sense of togetherness, living in an area or country dominated by a different culture

executive committee small group of people who control a political party, company or other organization

exodus departure of a large group of people from a country or area

feminist follower of a movement that developed throughout the 20th century, aiming to bring about financial and social equality for women

genocide killing of large numbers of people on the basis of their nationality or race

ghetto area of a town or city where a particular group of people – often an ethnic minority – live together

gypsies European name for the Roma, an ethnic group who originally came from northern India and now live in many parts of Europe

Haganah secret underground Jewish army founded in 1920 to defend Jews against Arab attacks

Hebrew original ancient language of the Jews, revived in the 20th century as the official language of Israel

Histadrut Jewish national labour union, founded in 1920 to help Jewish settlers in Palestine find work

Holocaust mass torture and extermination of Jews and other minorities carried out by the Nazi regime in Europe in the 1930s and 1940s

homeland area of land which an ethnic group or nation sees as its rightful home

immigration moving into one country from another to live there permanently

kibbutz Israeli communal farm

Knesset Israeli parliament

Labour Party Israeli political party (previously known as the Mapai Party) of which Golda Meir was the leader when she came to power in 1969

Mapai Party Israeli socialist political party founded in 1930, and dominant in the process of making Israel an independent state. After splitting, it reformed as part of the Labour Party in 1968.

Messiah according to Jewish tradition, this figure will be a descendant of King David who will deliver the Jews from suffering, end the Jewish exile and reign over a new kingdom of Israel

minority small group within a larger group or nation

Muslim follower of Islam and Mohammed the prophet

mutiny rebellion by the crew against the captain of a ship

nationalization process of taking over industries and resources so that they are owned and run by a country as a whole, instead of by private companies

Nazi Party National Socialist Party, led by Adolf Hitler, which came to power in Germany in 1933 and promoted prejudice against and persecution of Jews and other minorities

Ottoman Empire large area covering parts of Europe, Africa and Asia, controlled by the Turks for several hundred years before being dismantled after World War One

Palestine Liberation Organization (PLO) group set up by several Arab states in 1964 to oppose the state of Israel and help Palestinian Arabs fight to establish their own state

peninsula finger of land reaching out into the sea

persecution ill-treatment or harassment of a person or group, especially on the basis of their race or religion

pogrom type of organized riot, common in late 19th-century Russia, in which mobs rampaged through Jewish areas, killing Jews and destroying their property

press conference meeting where politicians or other newsworthy people talk to journalists and give them news

Promised Land Jewish name for Palestine, the part of the Middle East from which the Jews originally came and which, according to Jewish beliefs, God had promised to them

right wing in politics, tending towards conservative values of the importance of tradition and the power of the individual, rather than the state

skirmishes short battles

sniper gunman who fires shots from a hidden position

socialism political system originally based on equality and the fair distribution of a country's wealth among its people

socialist someone who believes in the equal distribution of wealth among the members of a society

steerage cheapest quarters on a passenger liner, usually located on the lower decks at the back of the ship

telegram early type of long distance communication, transmitted by sending electrical signals along cables

terrorism using or threatening violent attacks in an attempt to win political change

Tsar traditional monarch in pre-1917 Russia

tuberculosis infectious disease, usually of the lungs

unanimous completely one-sided with everyone in agreement

underground army or political group that operates in secret

United Nations (UN) international organization set up at the end of World War Two in 1945 to encourage peace and communication between the nations of the world

Va'ad Hapoel ruling committee of the Histadrut

Watergate scandal scandal that hit the US president, Richard Nixon in 1972 when it was discovered that members of his party had burgled the offices of their opponents and stolen important papers

White Paper official British government report or proposal on a particular issue

Yiddish traditional Jewish language spoken by many Jews in different parts of the world

Yishuv Jewish settlement in Palestine before independence

Zionism belief in the creation of a Jewish homeland

Zionist follower of Zionism

Index